A Visit to the Vet

by **Aubre Andrus**   photos by **Linda Kuo**

SCHOLASTIC INC.

For my daughter, Maggie, and
our beloved dogs, Tusker and Ernie.
–Linda Kuo

Photo credits: The photographs in this book were taken at locations including the New England Veterinary Medical Center (Mystic, CT): cover, title page, 1, 3, 5, 11, 13, 18, 27–29; Pound Ridge Veterinary Center (Pound Ridge, NY): 6, 9–10, 14, 17, 19–20, 22–23, 31; and the Center for Avian and Exotic Medicine (New York, NY): 7–8, 15–16, 24–26, 30. Additional icons © Thinkstock: 21: Askold Romanov; 16: ctrlaplus1; 8, 9, 13 left, 19, 23 left, 28: da-vooda; 5 left: sjhaytov; 5 right, 7, 11, 13 right, 15, 17, 18, 23 right, 25, 26, 29 left, 29 bottom, 29 right, 32: vectorikart.

The photographer wishes to thank the veterinarian clinics and their staff for their help and participation during this project. Special thanks go to Dr. Laurel Kaddatz, Dr. Cynthia Brown, Practice Manager Lorelei D'Avolio, technician Jenny Tkacz, and Sharon Okenquist, whose dedication, support, and generosity made it all possible.

Library of Congress Cataloging-in-Publication Data
Names: Andrus, Aubre, author. | Kuo, Linda, illustrator.
Title: A Visit to the Vet / by Aubre Andrus; photos by Linda Kuo.
Other titles: Scholastic reader. Level 2.
Description: New York, NY: Scholastic Inc., [2017] | Series: Scholastic reader level 2 | Audience: Ages 6–8. | Audience: K to grade 5.
Identifiers: LCCN 2016039835 | ISBN 9781338087611 (pbk.)
Subjects: LCSH: Veterinarians—Juvenile literature. | Veterinary Hospitals—Juvenile literature. | Veterinary medicine—Juvenile literature.
Classification: LCC SF756 .A53 2017 | DDC 636.089092–dc23
LC record available at https://lccn.loc.gov/2016039835

ISBN 978-1-338-08761-1

10 9 8 7 6 5 4 3 2 1   17 18 19 20 21

Printed in the USA   40
First printing, February 2017

Book design by Kay Petronio

Animals have to go to the doctor just like humans do! But they can't go to just any doctor. Animals go to a veterinarian. A veterinarian, or a "vet," is a special kind of doctor who cares for animals. Vets know how to keep all kinds of animal **species** healthy, from dogs to elephants and every animal in between!

It's really important that animals of all sizes get **wellness** checkups. Some vets will travel to an animal's home to take care of it. For example, a vet may visit a farm to check on the cows or horses that live there. Or a vet may travel to an animal **sanctuary** to visit large animals like hippos, tigers, and bears. That's because most veterinarian **clinics** are only for small pets like dogs, cats, rabbits, and gerbils.

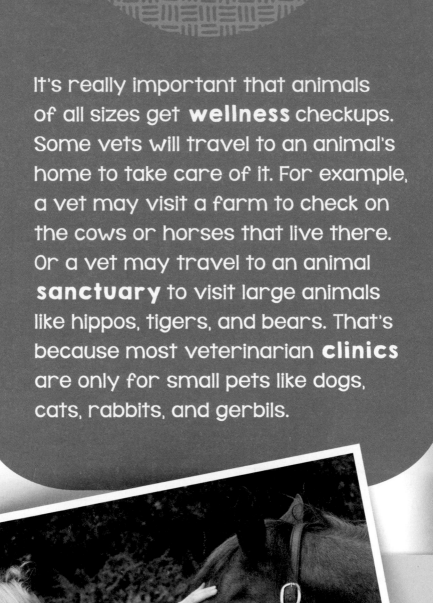

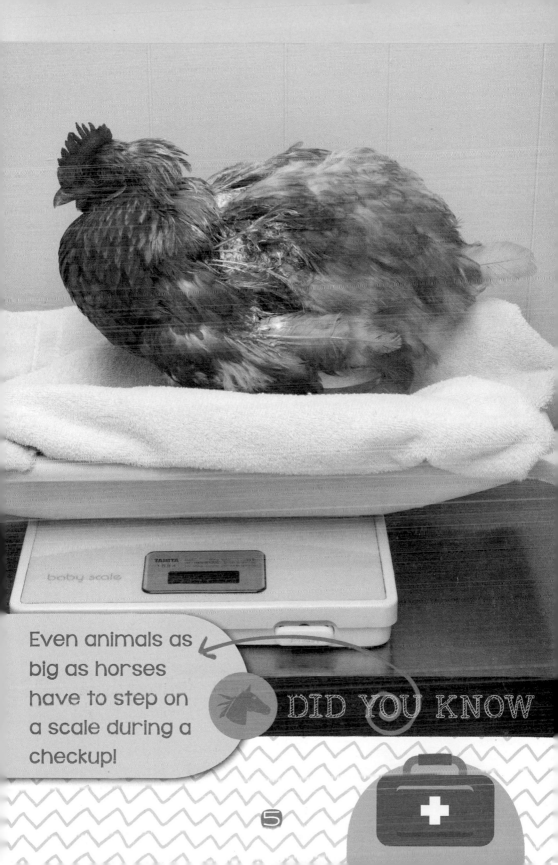

Even animals as big as horses have to step on a scale during a checkup!

DID YOU KNOW

You can see all kinds of small animals in the waiting room of a veterinary clinic. Owners keep their pets on leashes or in carriers so their pets stay close and feel safe. Many veterinary clinics have separate waiting areas for cats and dogs. And some clinics are either for dogs only or for cats only—after all, dogs and cats don't always get along!

Since animals can't talk, vets have to make **observations**. During an **examination**, vets look closely and carefully at the fur, feathers, skin, or scales of their patient. They feel all around the animal's body to make sure everything seems normal.

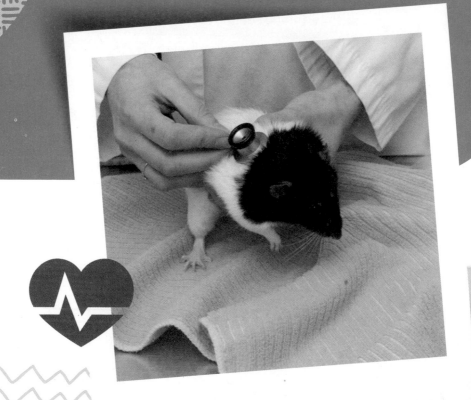

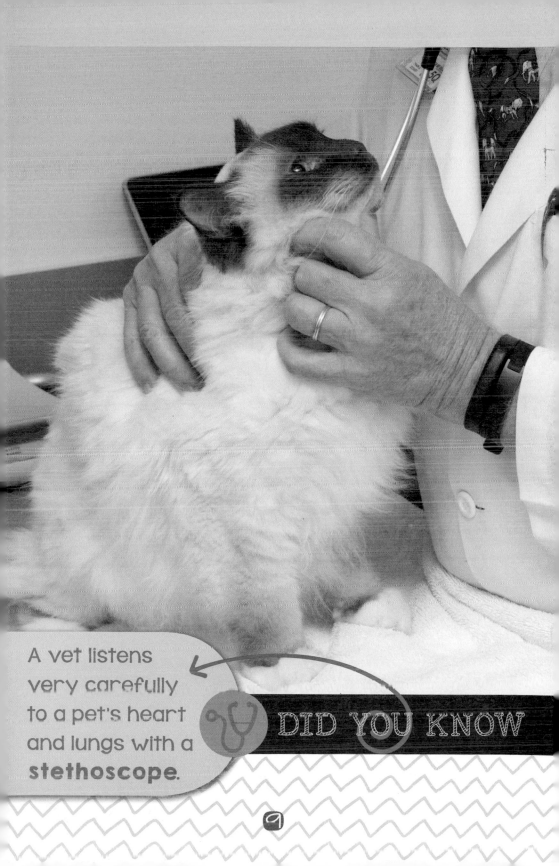

A vet listens very carefully to a pet's heart and lungs with a **stethoscope**.

DID YOU KNOW

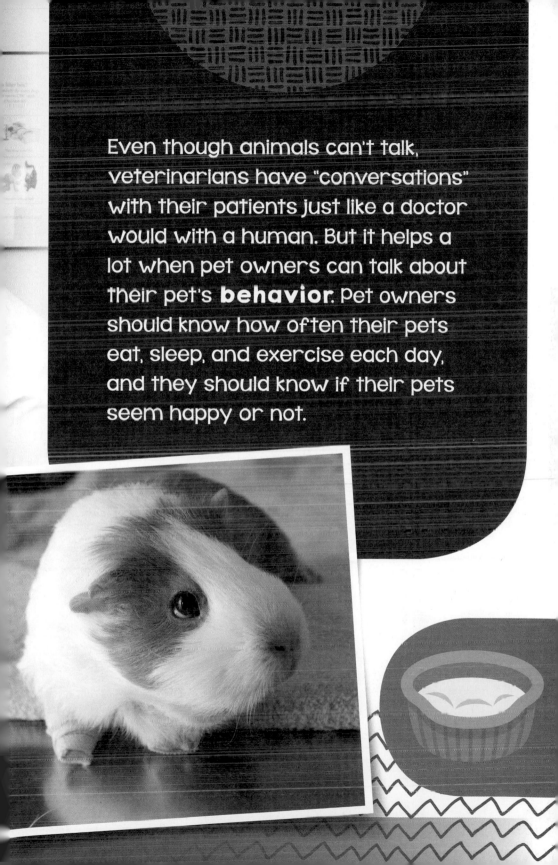

Even though animals can't talk, veterinarians have "conversations" with their patients just like a doctor would with a human. But it helps a lot when pet owners can talk about their pet's **behavior.** Pet owners should know how often their pets eat, sleep, and exercise each day, and they should know if their pets seem happy or not.

Just like humans, animals need regular checkups throughout their lives. At a typical appointment, vets check the pet's ears, eyes, teeth, and heartbeat. Sometimes the vet will suggest a **vaccination**. Vaccinations are shots of special medicine that help keep animals and people from getting certain sicknesses. The vet may give treats to make the pet feel less scared, especially after a shot.

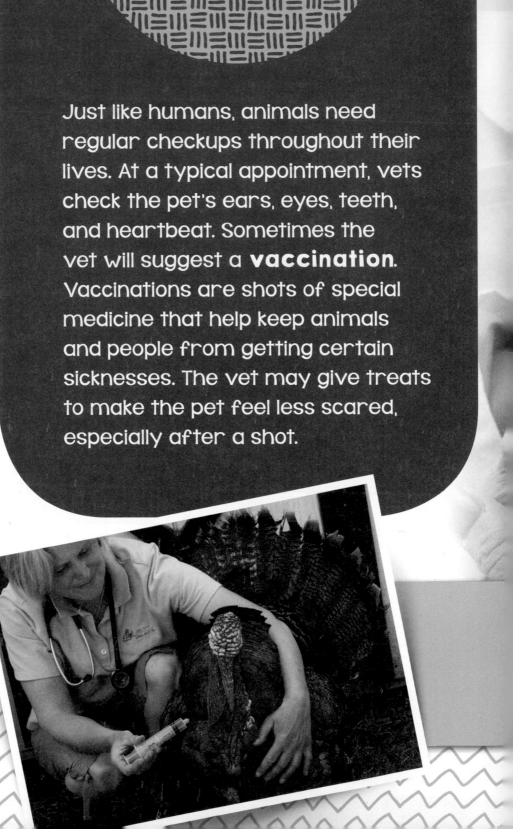

Adult animals should visit the vet once a year for a checkup.

DID YOU KNOW

Vets weigh pets at each appointment. A pet's weight can tell the vet whether or not the pet is exercising enough or getting the right amount of food. If a pet weighs too much or too little, a vet can give advice to the pet owner on how to keep their pet happy and healthy.

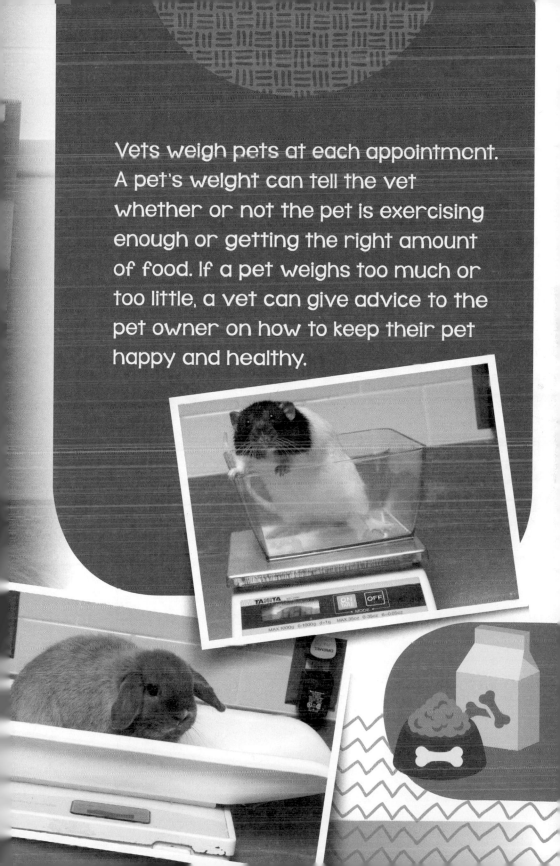

Puppies and kittens can be fed milk with special bottles if they need help growing.

DID YOU KNOW

Different kinds of pets eat different kinds of foods, and they all have their own eating schedules. Animals often eat more when they are young and growing and less as they get older. Your vet can teach you what your pet should be eating, as well as how much and how often it should eat.

Animals can't eat without healthy teeth. Puppies lose baby teeth just like humans. They may not brush their teeth every night before bed, but they can chew on bones and treats that can help keep their teeth clean. Vets like to check animals' teeth during wellness visits just like a dentist would.

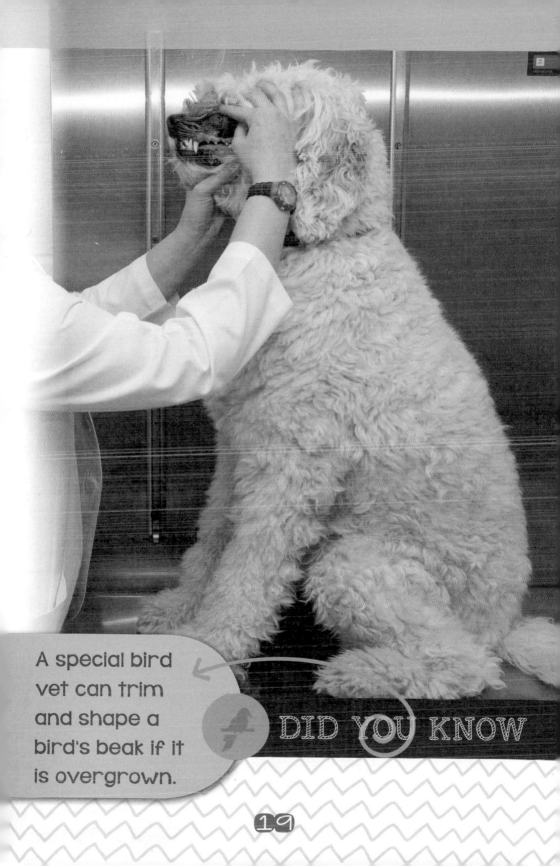

A special bird vet can trim and shape a bird's beak if it is overgrown.

DID YOU KNOW

Pets don't wear glasses, but it is still important for them to get their eyes checked. Some vets even specialize in animal eye care. That is because pets don't always see the same way humans do. Dogs see fewer colors than people. In fact, vets believe that dogs cannot see the difference between similar shades of colors such as red or blue. A lot of things just look gray! Luckily, dogs make up for their eyesight by having a great sense of smell!

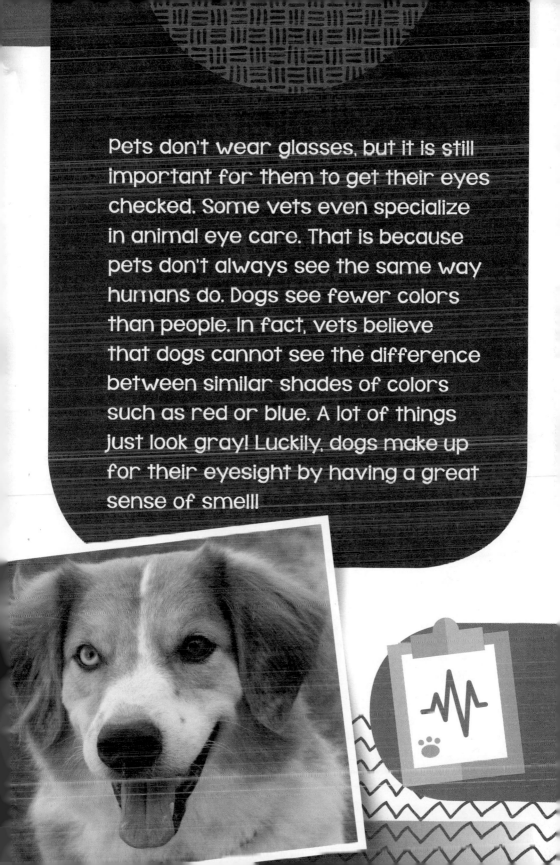

Most pets age faster than people. A large breed of dog can be considered old at only age 6 or 7. The vet might recommend a special diet or exercise plan for an older pet. A vet keeps a history of every pet's health to help the animal stay healthy and happy throughout its entire life.

The world's oldest dog—an Australian cattle dog named Bluey—lived to be 29 years old!

DID YOU KNOW

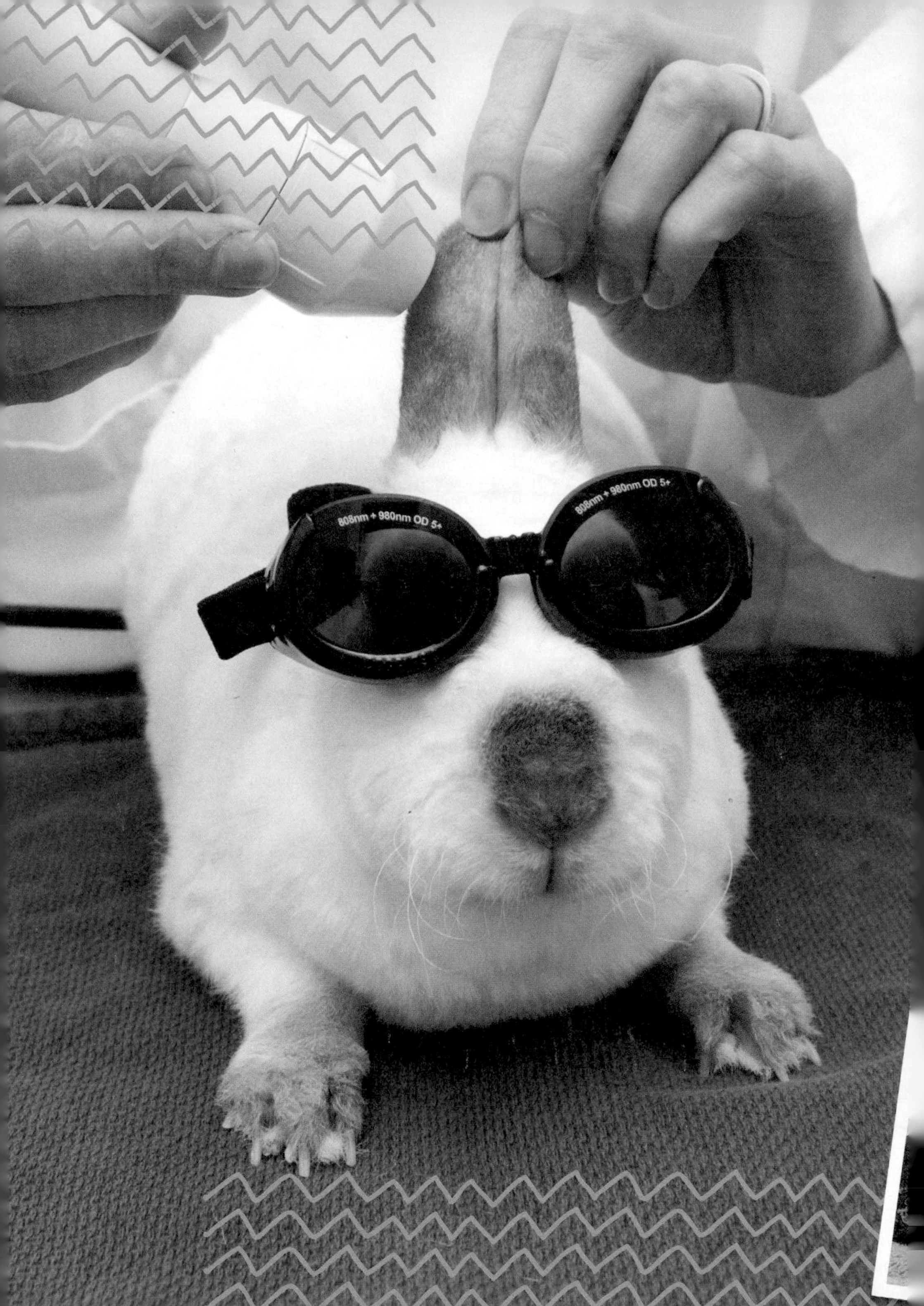
808nm + 980nm OD 5+
808nm + 980nm OD 5+

If an animal is sick or hurt, it can be taken to the veterinary hospital. There the vet may run a lab test on the animal's blood to help make a **diagnosis**. The vet might give **medication** to make the animal feel better. Or the pet may need to get an **X-ray** so the vet can see inside its body to figure out what is wrong. Based on the X-ray, the vet could decide to perform a **surgery**, set a broken bone back in place, or send the pet home with its family to get some rest.

If a pet needs surgery, some of the animal's fur is shaved first. That way, the vet can see the skin more easily. The vet will often use medication to help the animal sleep during the surgery so it cannot feel anything.

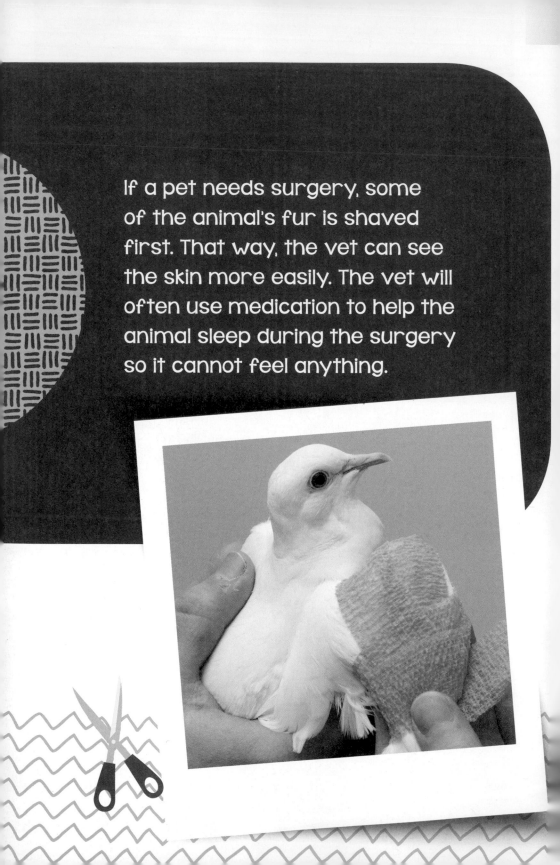

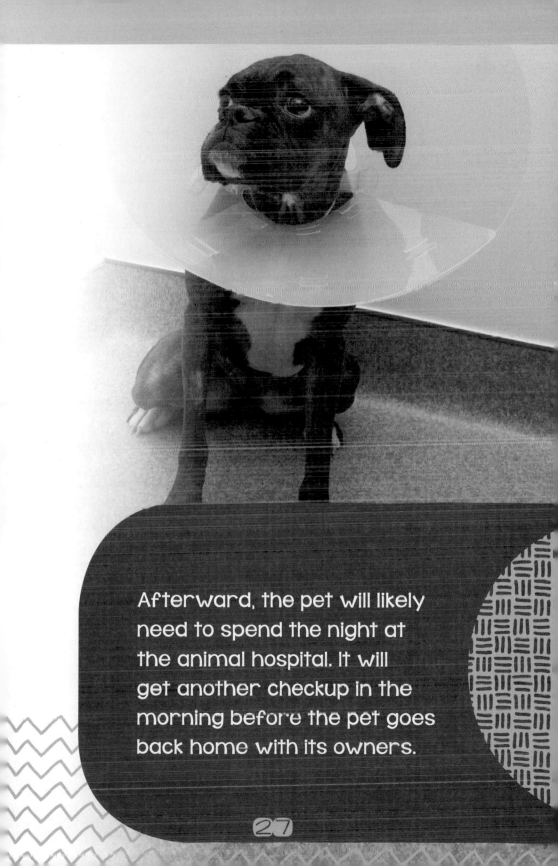

Afterward, the pet will likely need to spend the night at the animal hospital. It will get another checkup in the morning before the pet goes back home with its owners.

Dogs usually prefer to play with their BFF instead of in a large group.

DID YOU KNOW

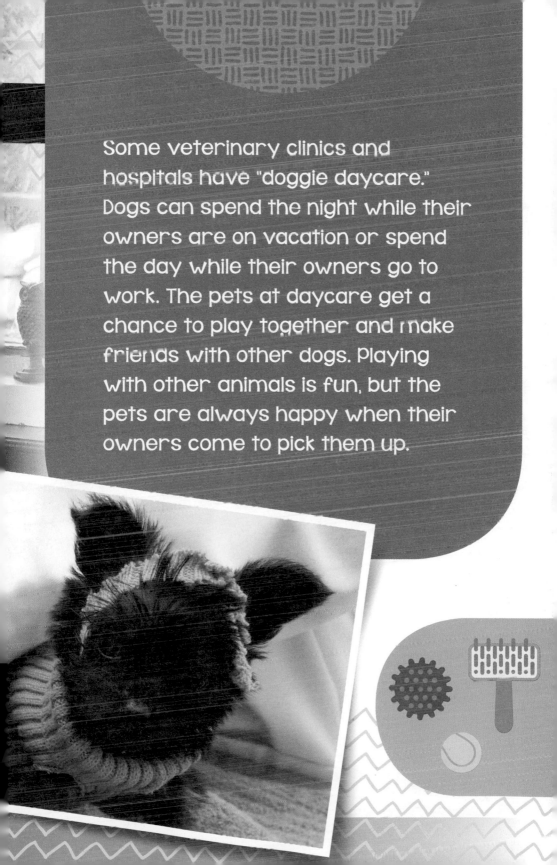

Some veterinary clinics and hospitals have "doggie daycare." Dogs can spend the night while their owners are on vacation or spend the day while their owners go to work. The pets at daycare get a chance to play together and make friends with other dogs. Playing with other animals is fun, but the pets are always happy when their owners come to pick them up.

Whether your pet is headed to the vet for a checkup, surgery, or an overnight stay, the vet is there to help. In fact, veterinarians are some of the biggest animal lovers out there. They give the best advice on how to keep your pet happy and healthy.

It doesn't matter if your pet is scaly or furry, big or small— vets love all pets!

GLOSSARY

behavior: how someone acts normally or in a certain situation

clinic: a hospital department where people receive medical treatment or advice

diagnosis: identification of the disease a patient has or what the cause of a problem is

examination: a careful check, especially of your body, by a doctor

medication: a substance used for treating an injury or illness

observation: something you have noticed by watching carefully

sanctuary: a natural area where animals are protected from hunters

species: one of the groups into which animals and plants are divided

stethoscope: a medical tool used by doctors and nurses to listen to sounds from the body

surgery: an operation performed by a doctor

vaccination: a shot that helps protect animals or humans against a disease

wellness: being healthy and happy

X-ray: a photo that shows the inside of the body, including bones and organs